The Animals of Paradise Coloring Book

Karima Sperling

Other Titles By This Author:

My Little Lore of Light
The Light of Muhammad
Links of Light: The Golden Chain
The Story of Moses
Who Are You? A Book of Very Serious Questions
The Animals of Paradise
The Animals of Paradise: Coloring Book
Every Day A Thousand Times

Printed in the United States of America ISBN 978-0-9913003-4-1

Little Bird Books littlebirdbooksink@gmail.com

The Camel of Prophet Salih (as)

In the eyes of the wise she glowed with the light of paradise. Her legs were studded with rubies, her chest was of spun gold, her hump was draped in a veil of jewels, her eyelashes shone with pearls, and over her head hung a diadem of stars.

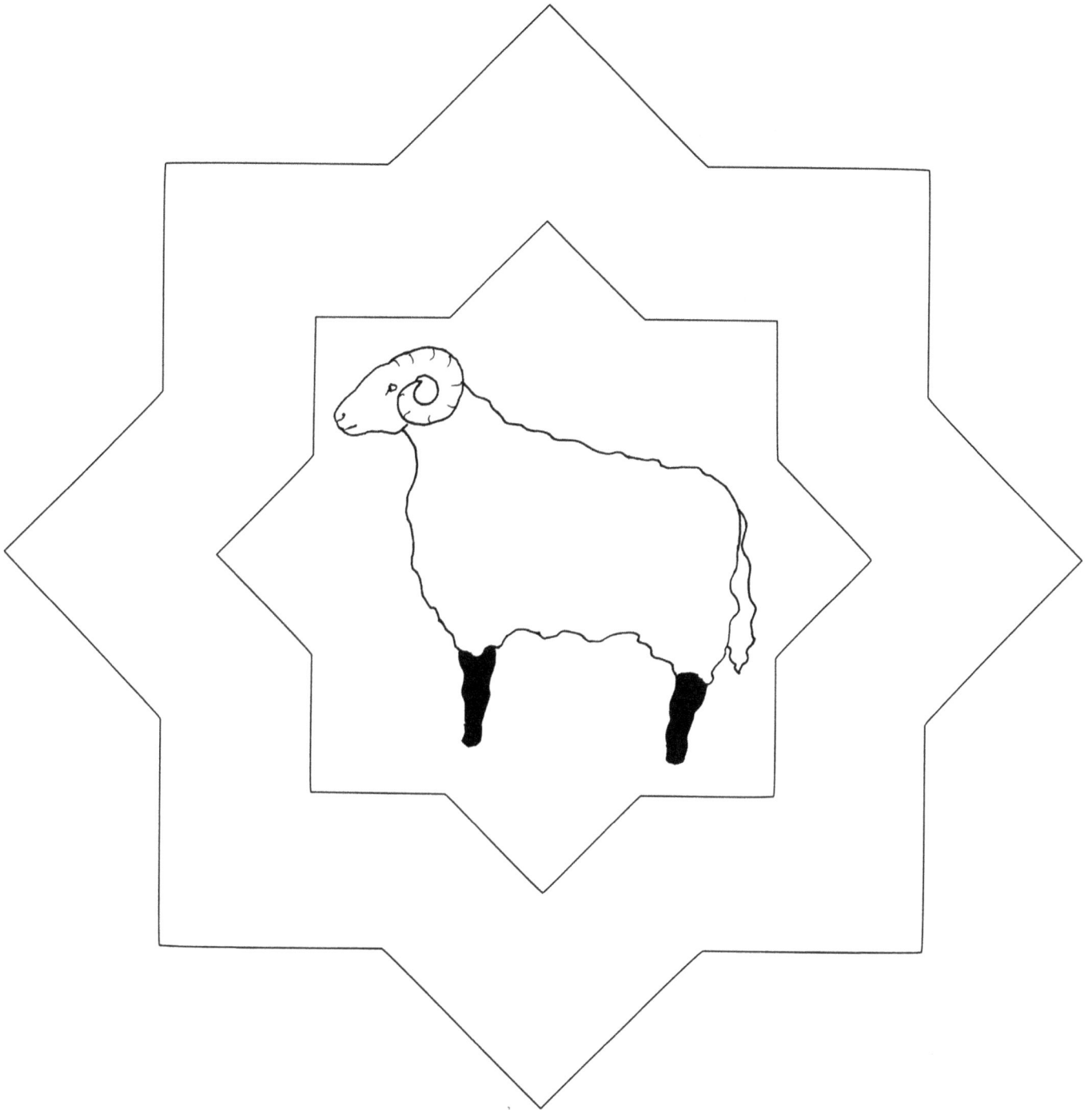

The Sheep of Prophet Isma'il (as)

He was chosen by Allah to take the place of the young prophet Isma'il and he was happy to fulfill his destiny by being sacrificed in Isma'il's place.

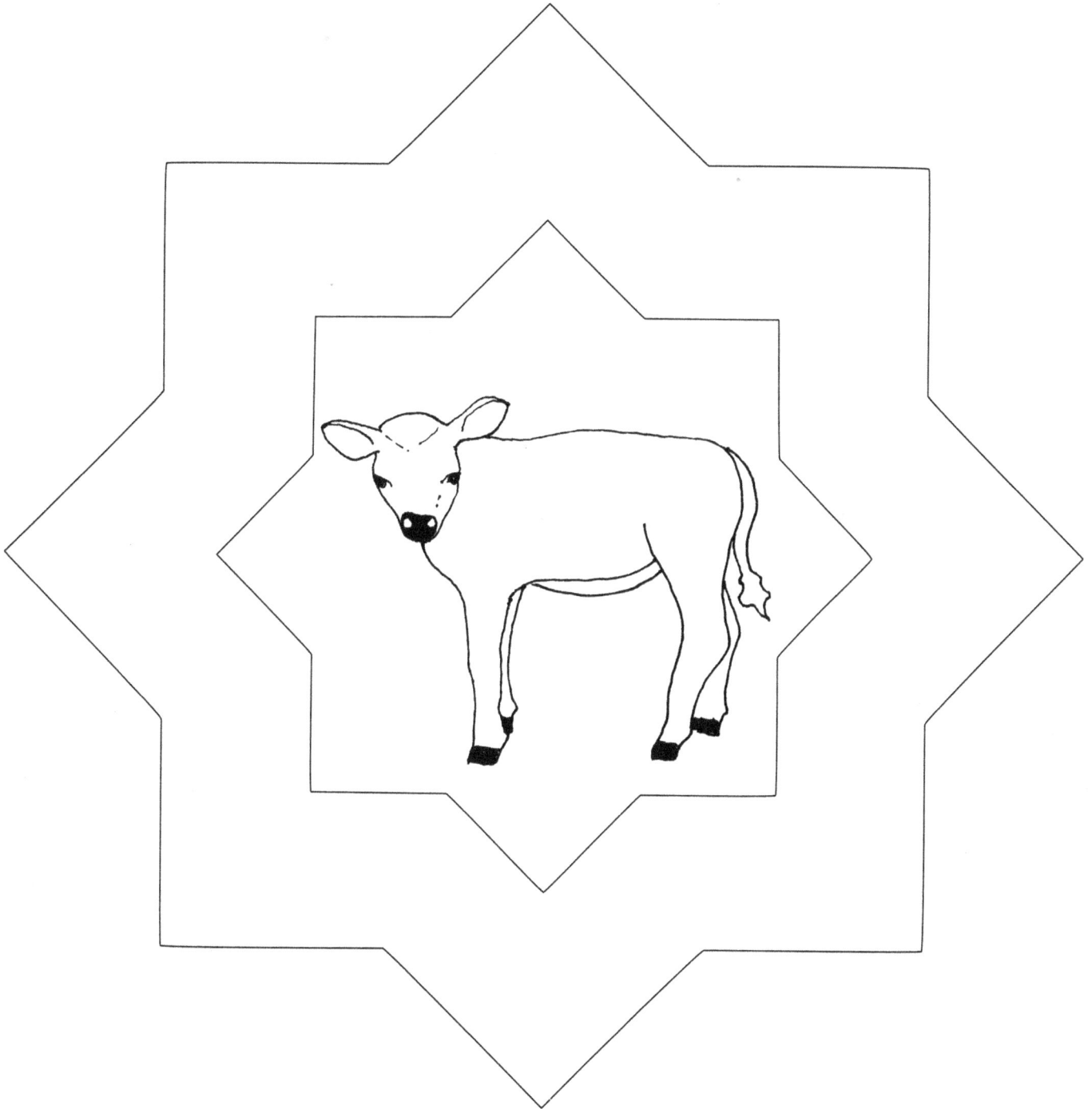

The Calf of Prophet Ibrahim (as)

He was a big, healthy animal, clean and bright. He was the pride of Sayyiduna Ibrahim and he was chosen to honor the angelic guests.

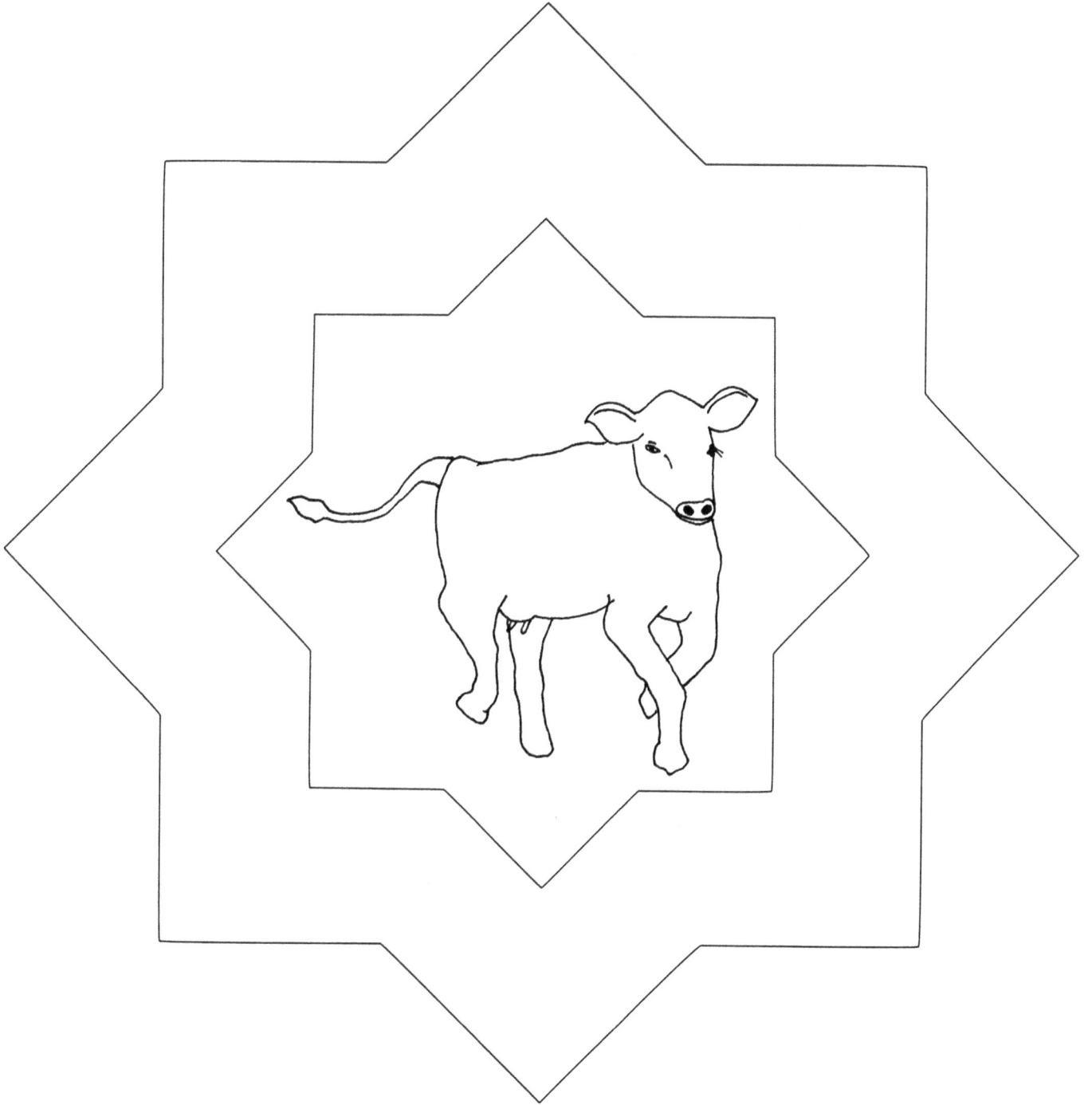

The Cow of Prophet Musa (as)

She was neither old nor young but in between. She was a bright yellow color that makes people happy. She had never worked in the fields and was without marks or scars. She was beautiful.

The Hudhud of
Prophet Sulayman (as)

The Hudhud had no fear because he carried the letter of his King and master and because on it was written, BismiLlahi r-Rahmani r-Rahim.

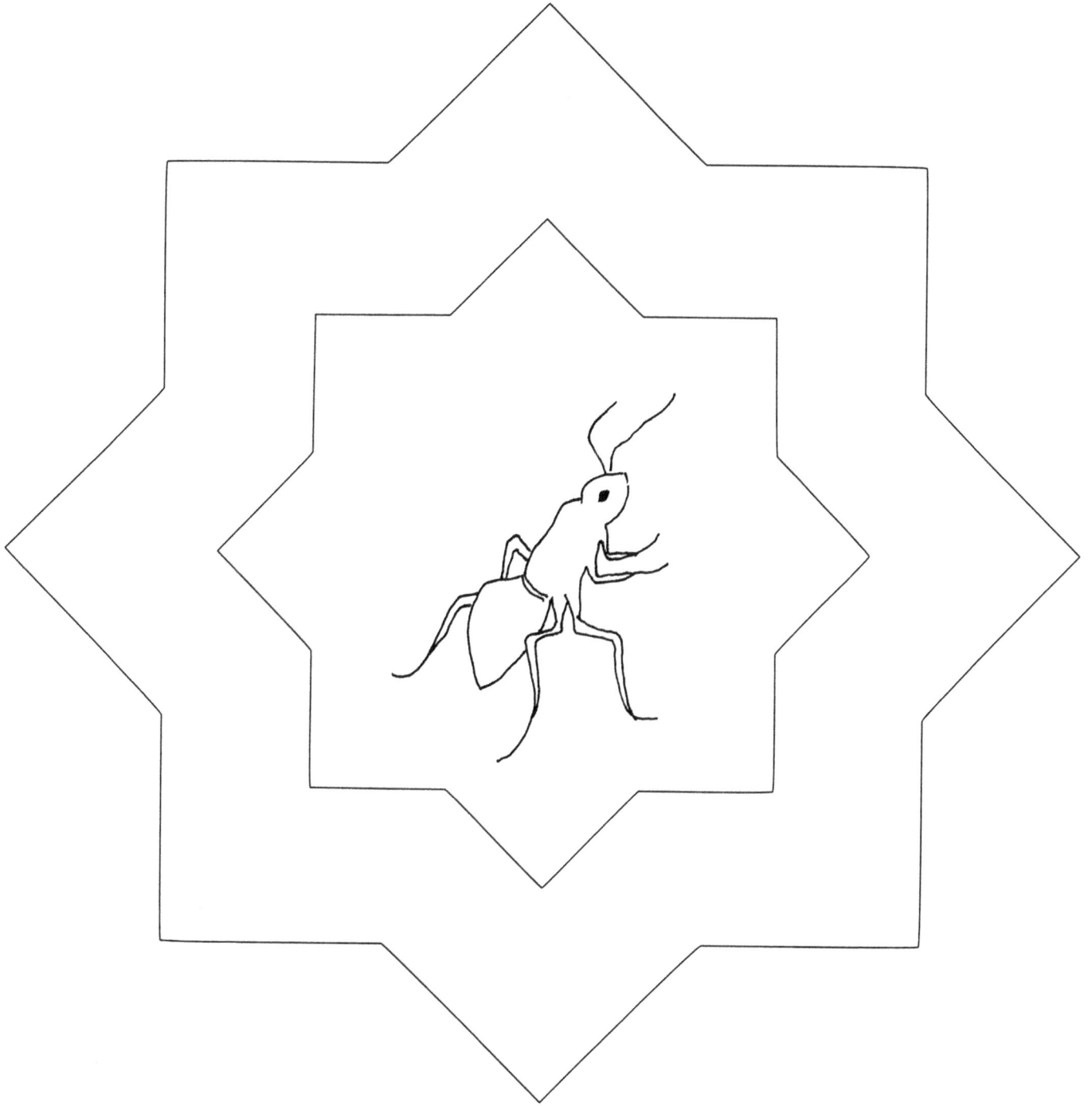

The Ant of Prophet Sulayman (as)

The little ant girl saved her people from being trampled by an army and saved the army from trampling the nation of ants.

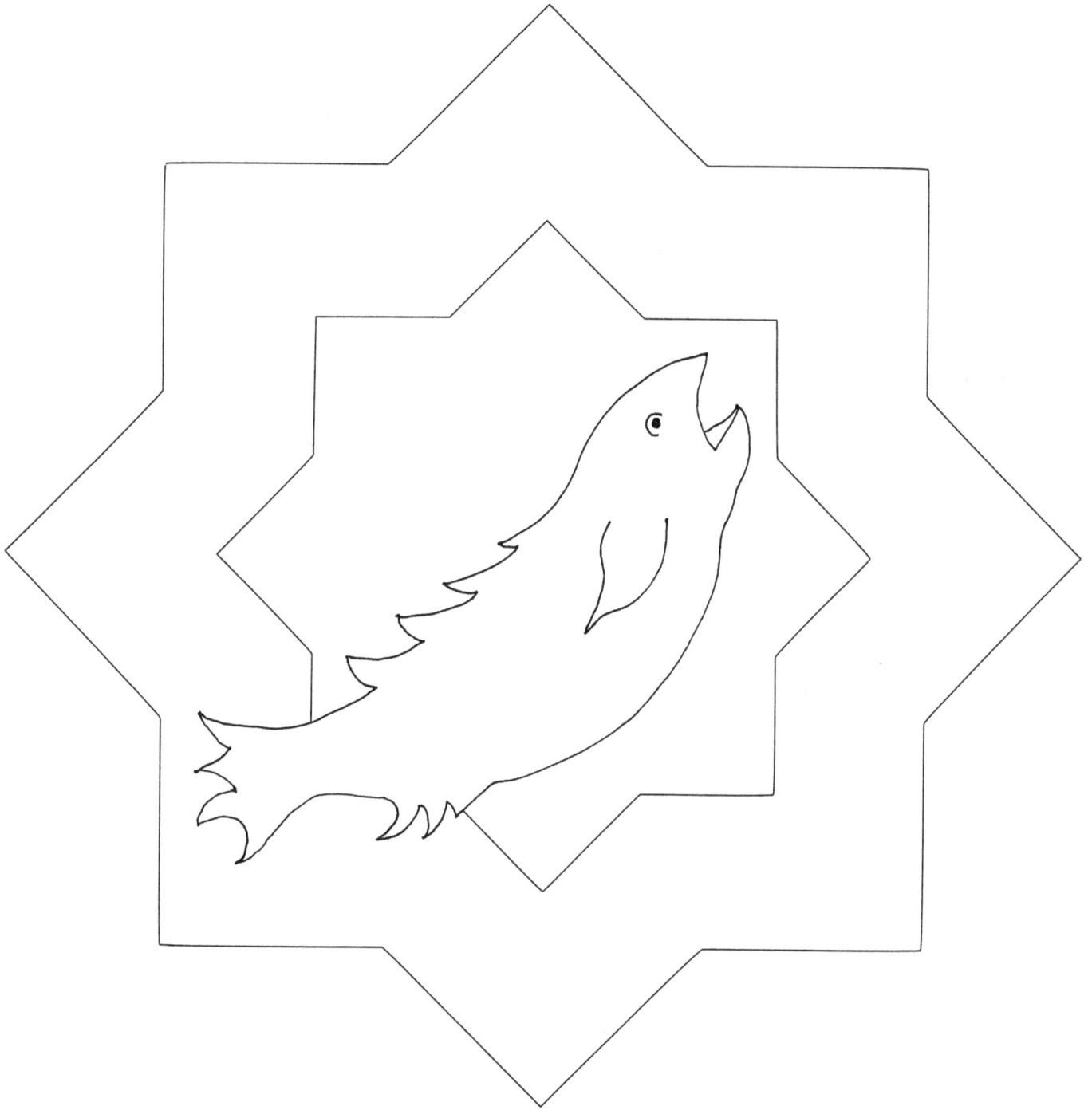

The Fish of Prophet Yunus (as)

Allah commanded the fish not to chew one bite of Yunus's flesh or break one bone of his body.
So the obedient fish swallowed him whole. In the belly of the fish Yunus praised Allah and the
fish praised with him.

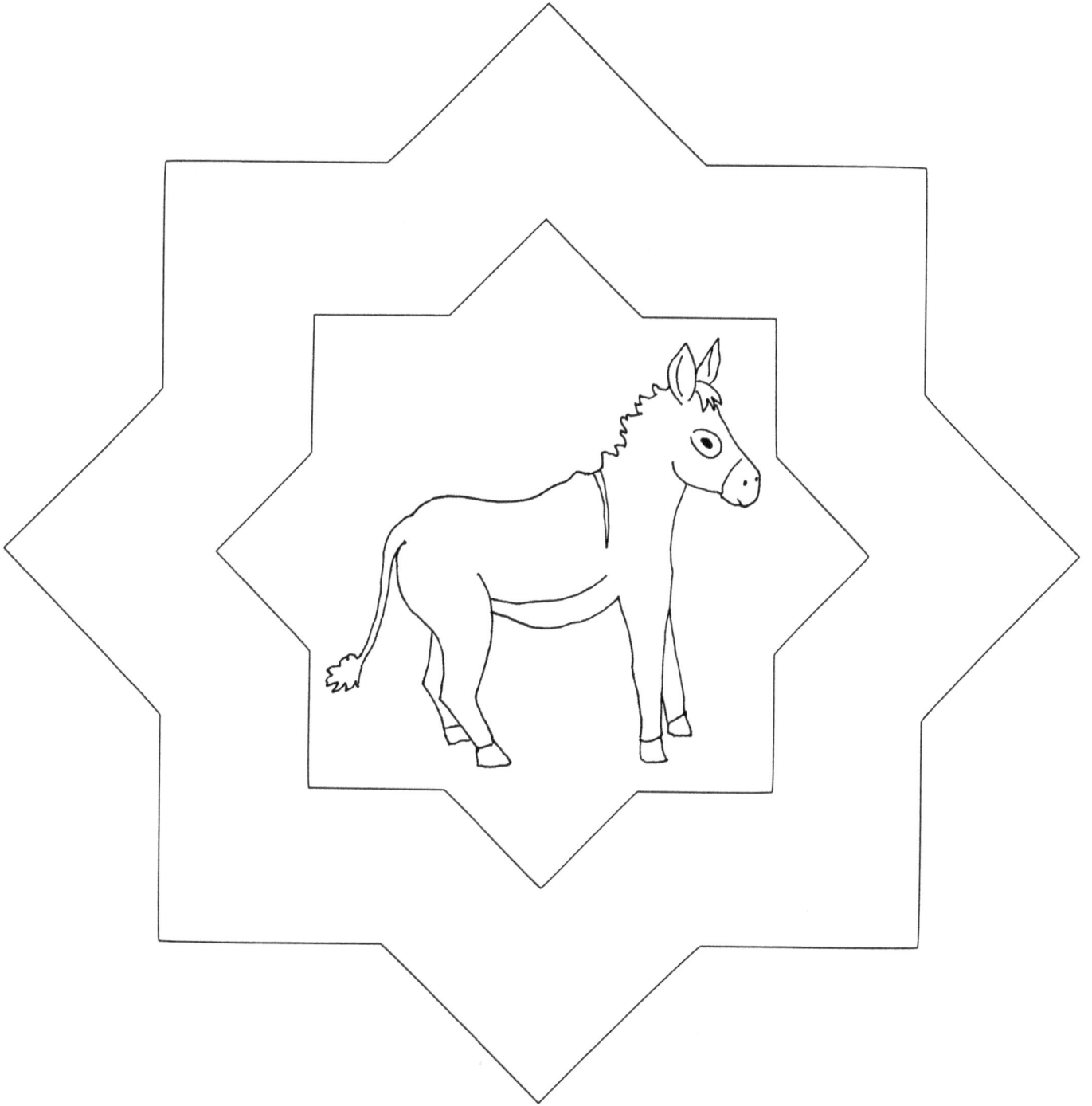

The Donkey of Prophet Uzair (as)

Before Uzair's startled eyes the little donkey shuddered as life began to flow in its body once more. It opened its eyes, stumbled to its feet and shook itself, swishing its tail and rippling its skin as donkeys do. After that it carried Uzair everywhere he went.

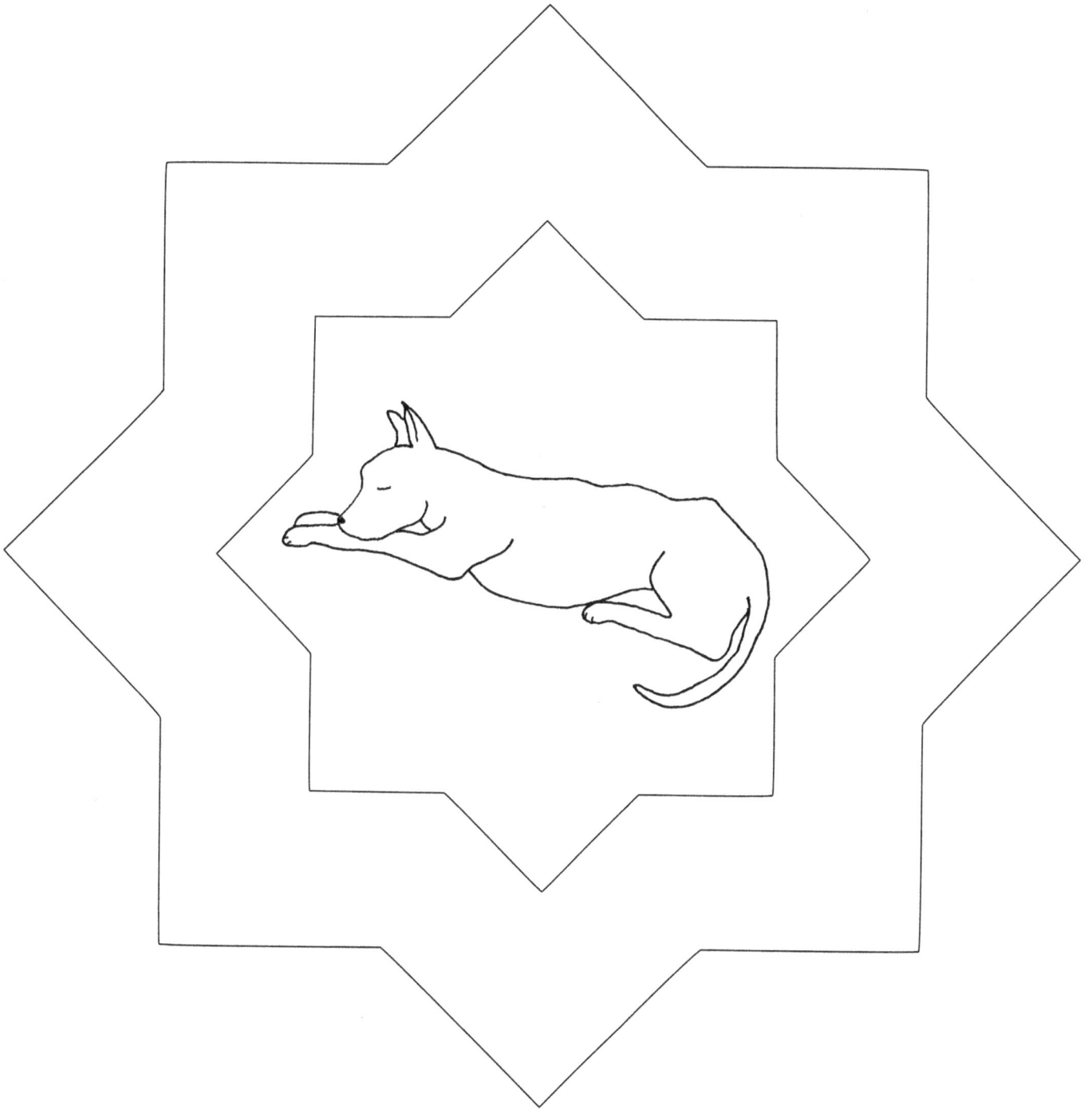

The Dog of the Seven Sleepers

Qitmir, the sheep dog, settled himself with determination across the mouth of the cave. He knew that his job was to guard the seven boys. He would let no one in.

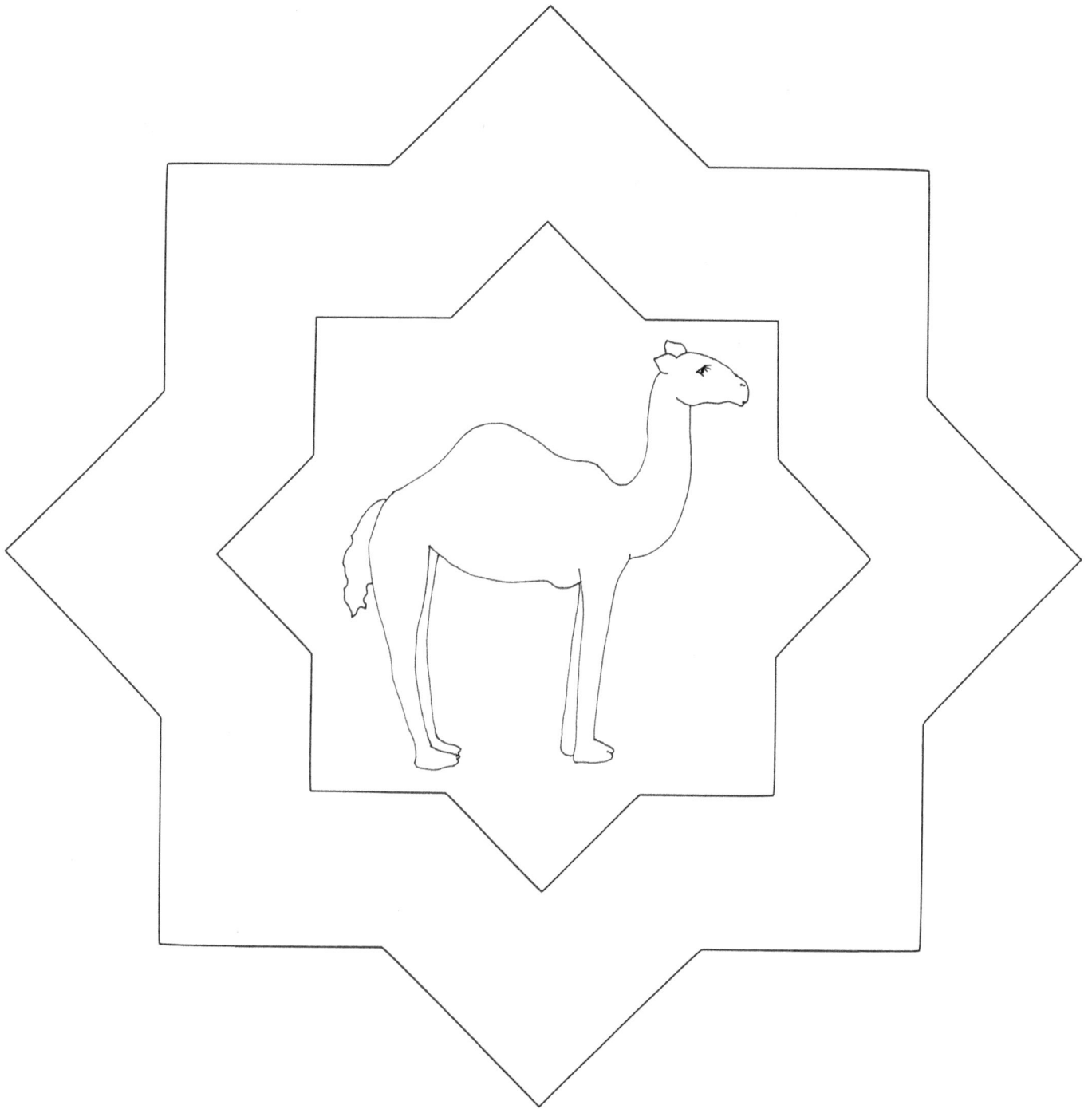

The Camel of Prophet Muhammad (sas)

She carried him safely and swiftly across both sand and stone to the farthest distances and she was divinely guided.

The Animals of Prophet Adam (as)

The snake and the peacock brought evil into the garden, tempting Adam and Hawwa to disobey their generous Lord. The swallow consoled them. The oxen helped them.

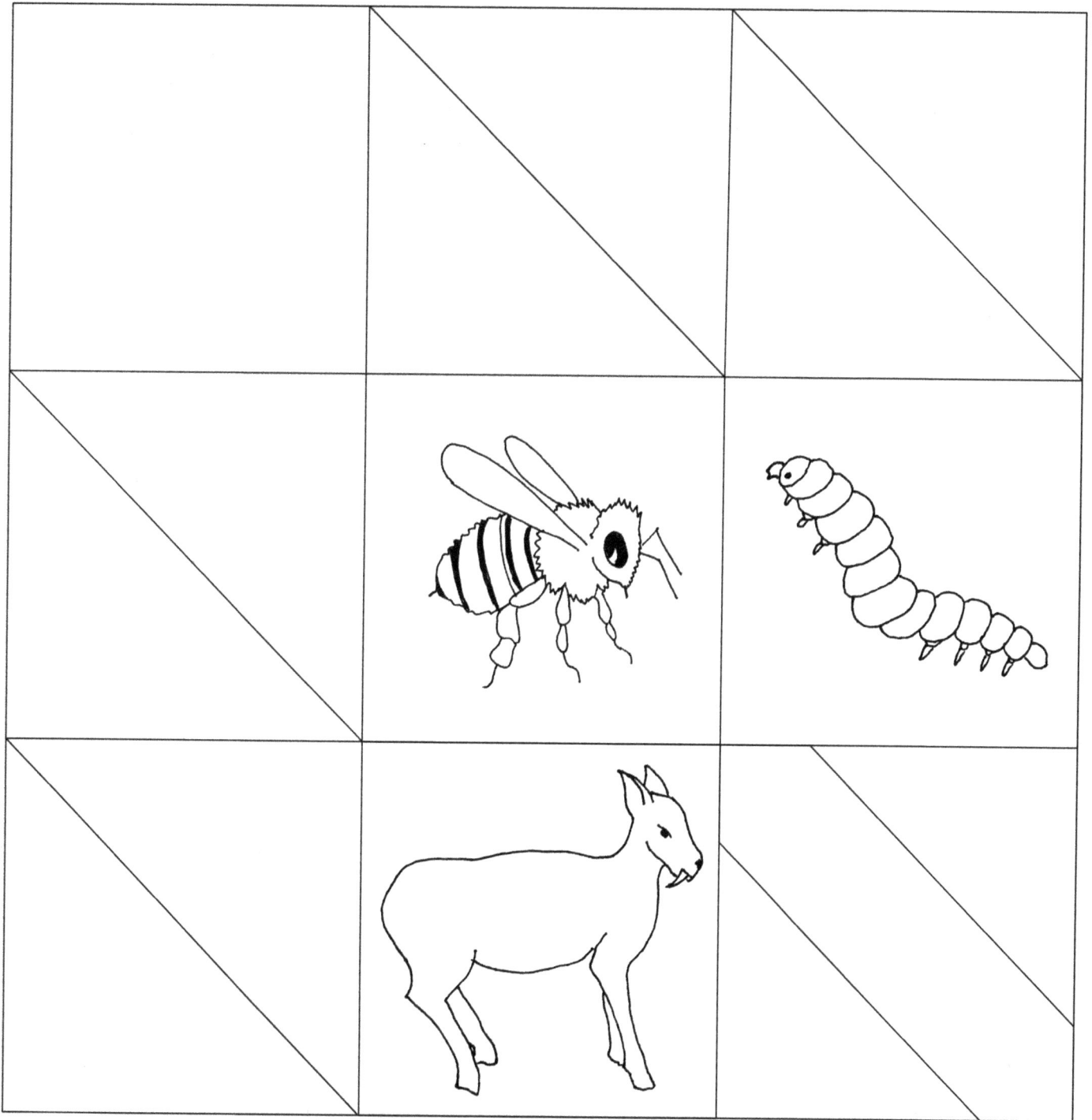

The Bee, the Worm, and the Deer of Prophet Adam (as)

They ate of the leaves of paradise and the bee began to make honey and the worm to make silk and the deer to make perfume.

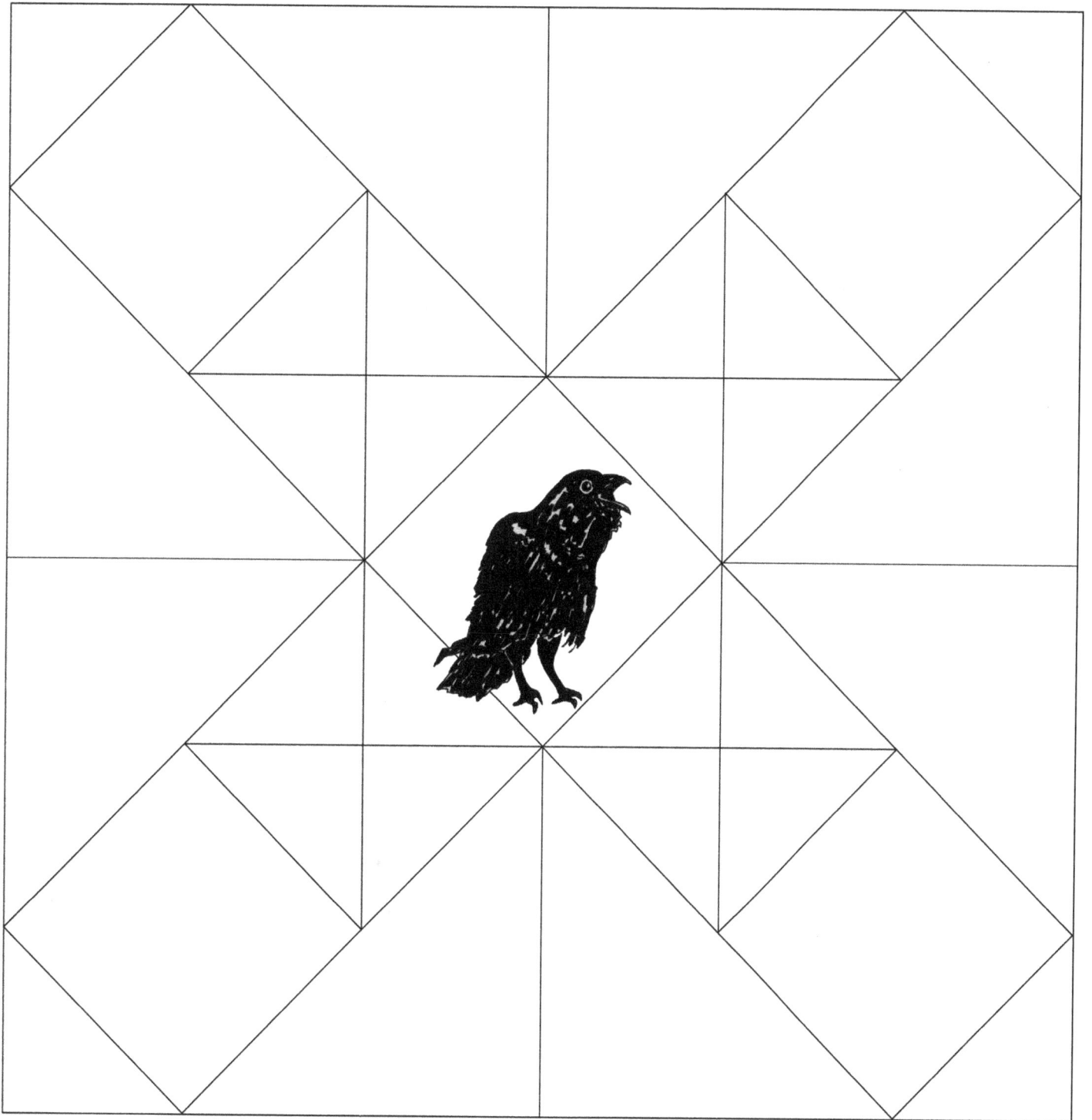

The Raven of Qabil

One day the raven had pity on Qabil and showed him how to bury his brother and Qabil recognized that even the rascally raven was wiser than he.

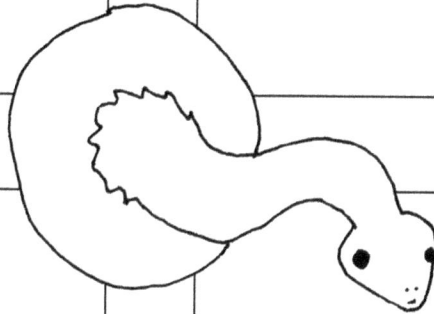

The Animals of the
Ark of Prophet Noah (as)

Allah commanded Noah to take a pair of each kind of animal on board the ark and they floated
in peace on the waters of Allah's anger.

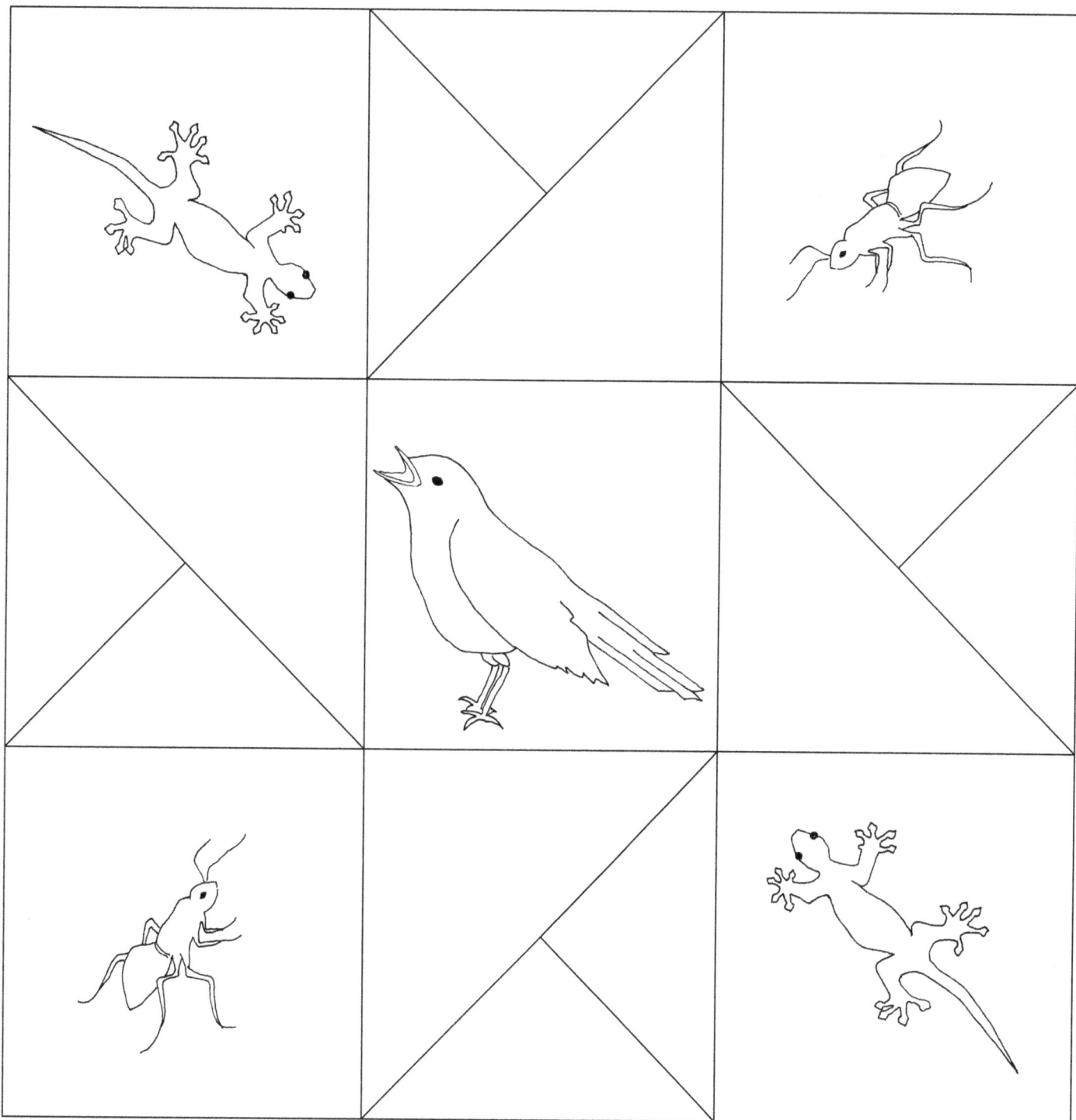

The Animals and the Fire
of Prophet Ibrahim (as)

All the animals, even the ant, came to the edge of the fire with whatever tiny amount of water they could carry in their mouths. The nightingale threw himself into the flames. Only the gecko tried to fan the flames higher.

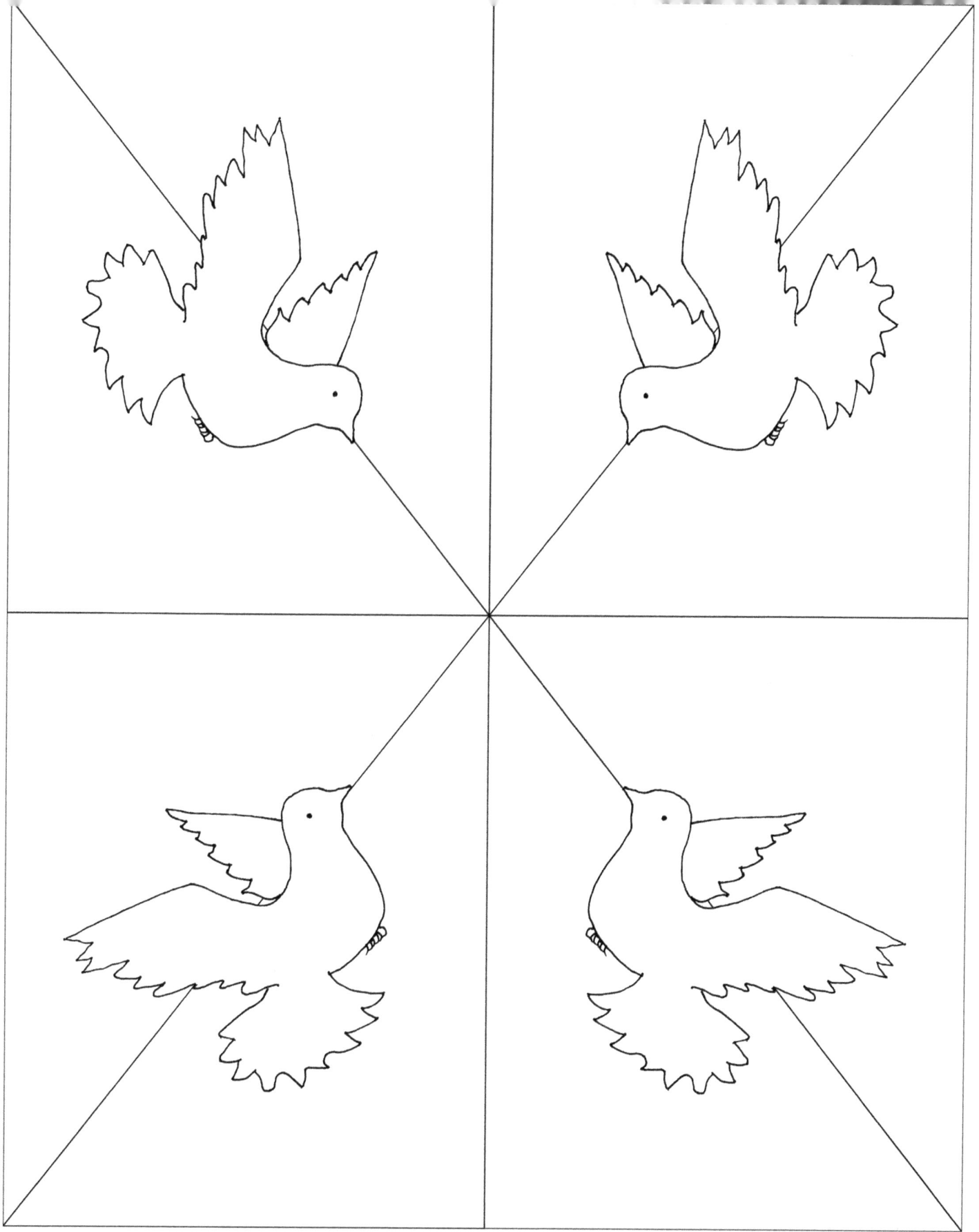

The Pigeons of Prophet Ibrahim (as)

The pigeons have only one goal, to spread their wings and head for home.

The Wolf of Prophet Yusuf (as)

The wolves know that Allah has forbidden them to harm the prophets.

The Fish of Prophet Musa (as)

The dried fish suddenly wriggled out of the lunch basket and leaped into the water.

The Worm and
Prophet Sulayman (as)

A little worm had been chewing away happily at Sulayman's wooden staff and had finally eaten it all the way through.

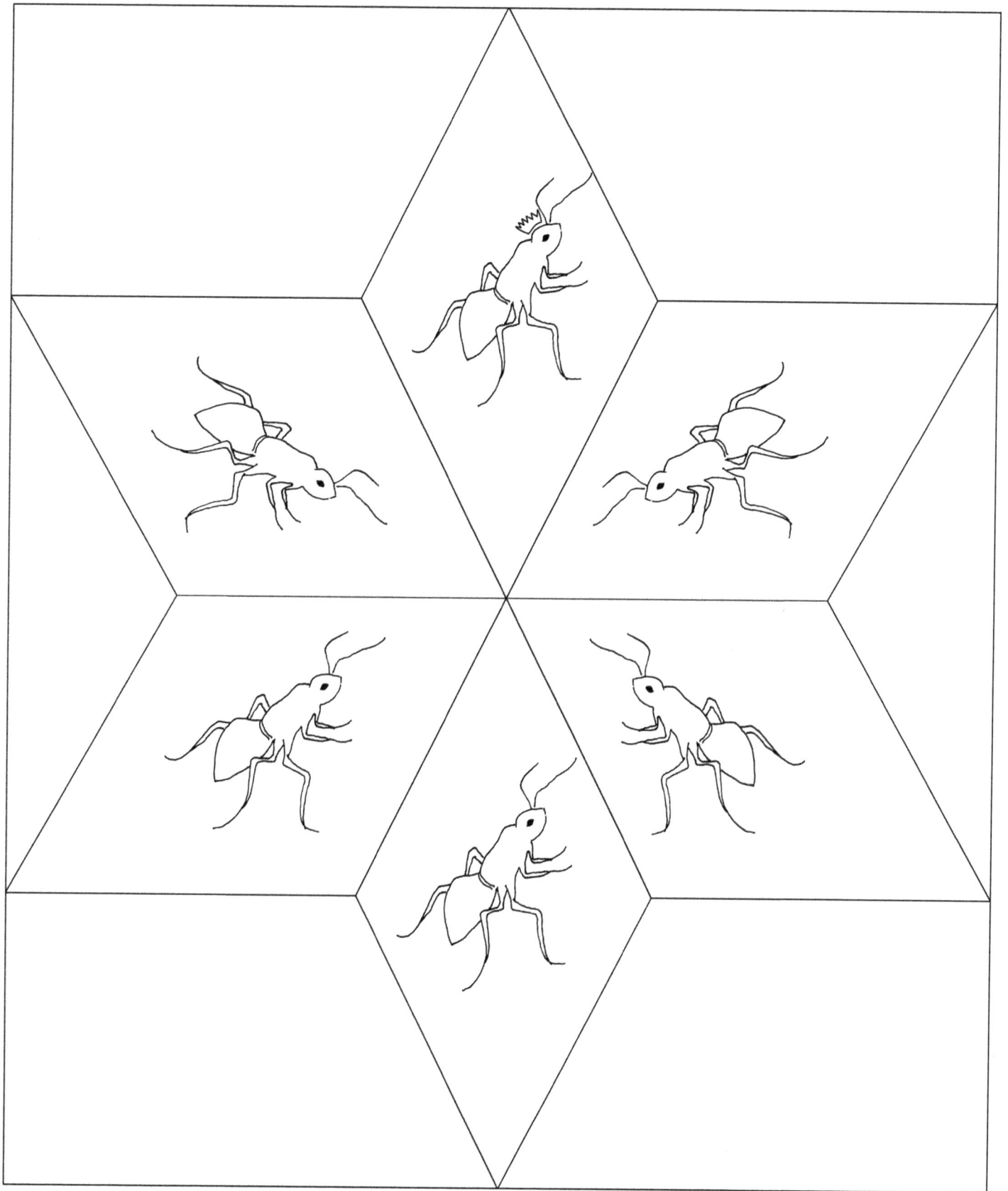

The Ants and Prophet Sulayman (as)

The tiny ants taught wisdom to the wisest prophet.

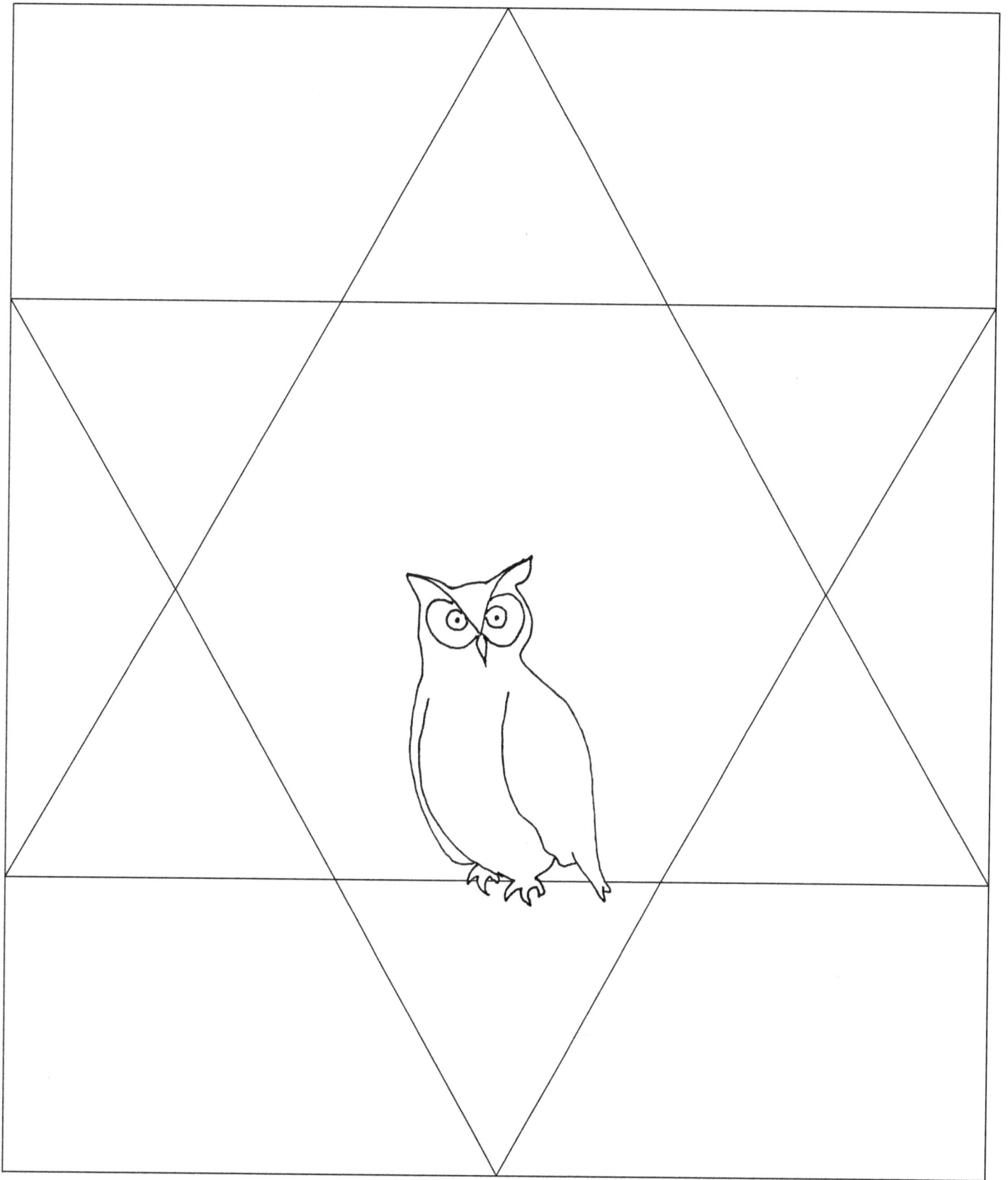

The Owl and the
Prophet Sulayman (as)

"Why" said the owl, "would I choose you as a friend O King Sulayman, when I have Allah as my Friend?"

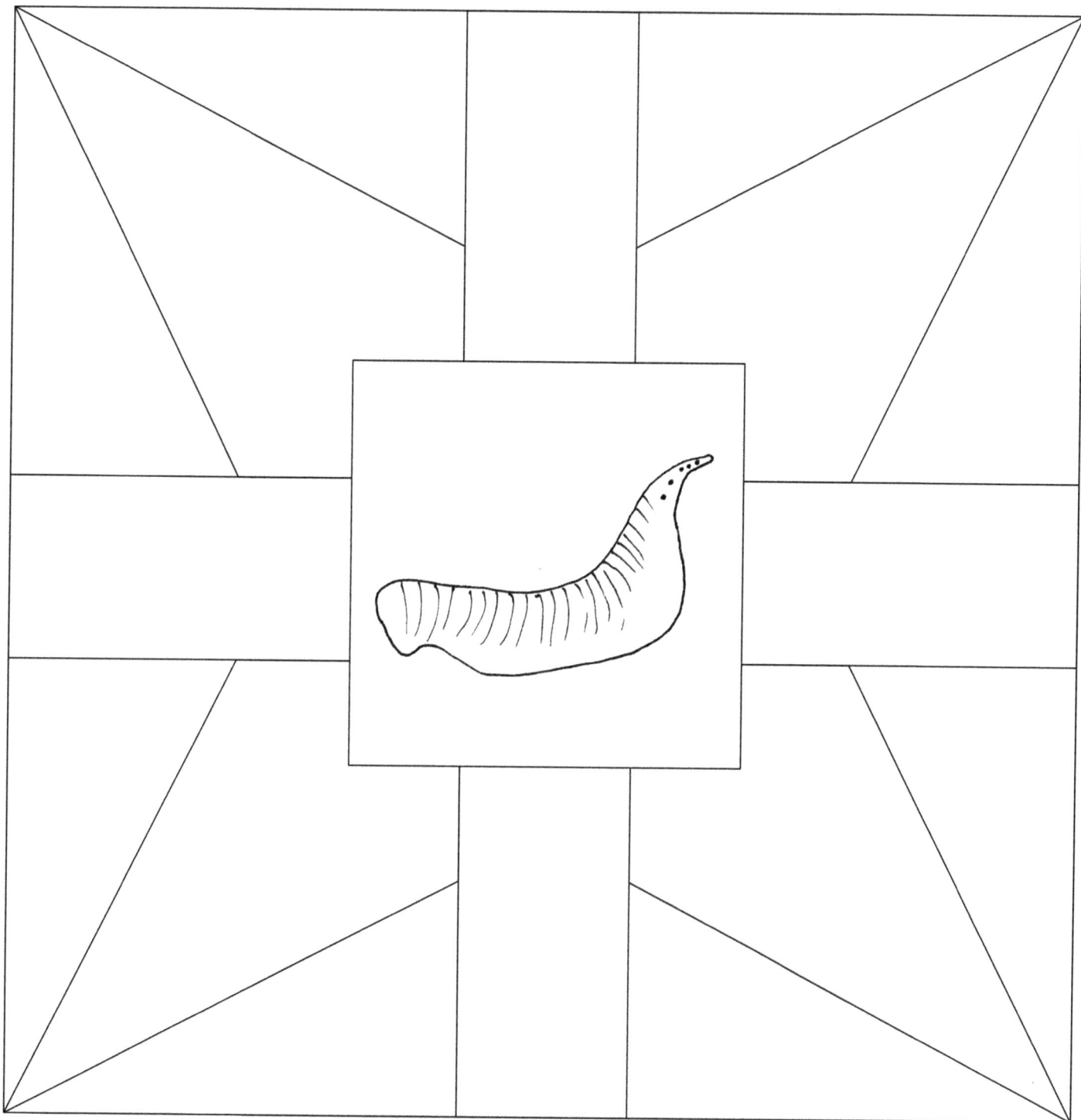

The Leech of Prophet Ayyub (as)

The ten-eyed medicinal leech is a sign of the love that Allah puts even in the things that are hard for us.

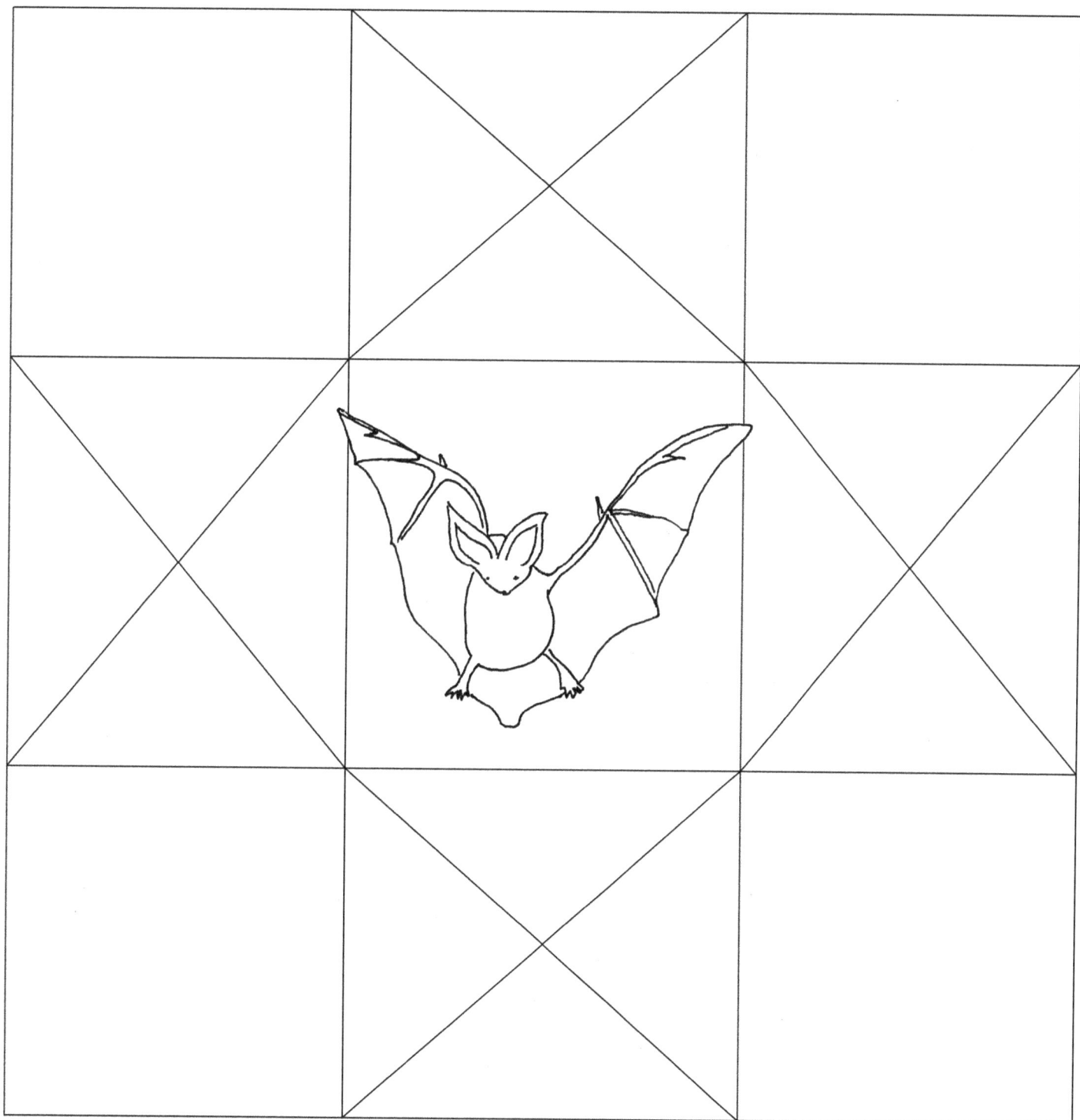

The Bat of Prophet Isa (as)

Sayyiduna Isa made a bird of clay and blew on it with Allah's name. The strange figure came to life as the bat.

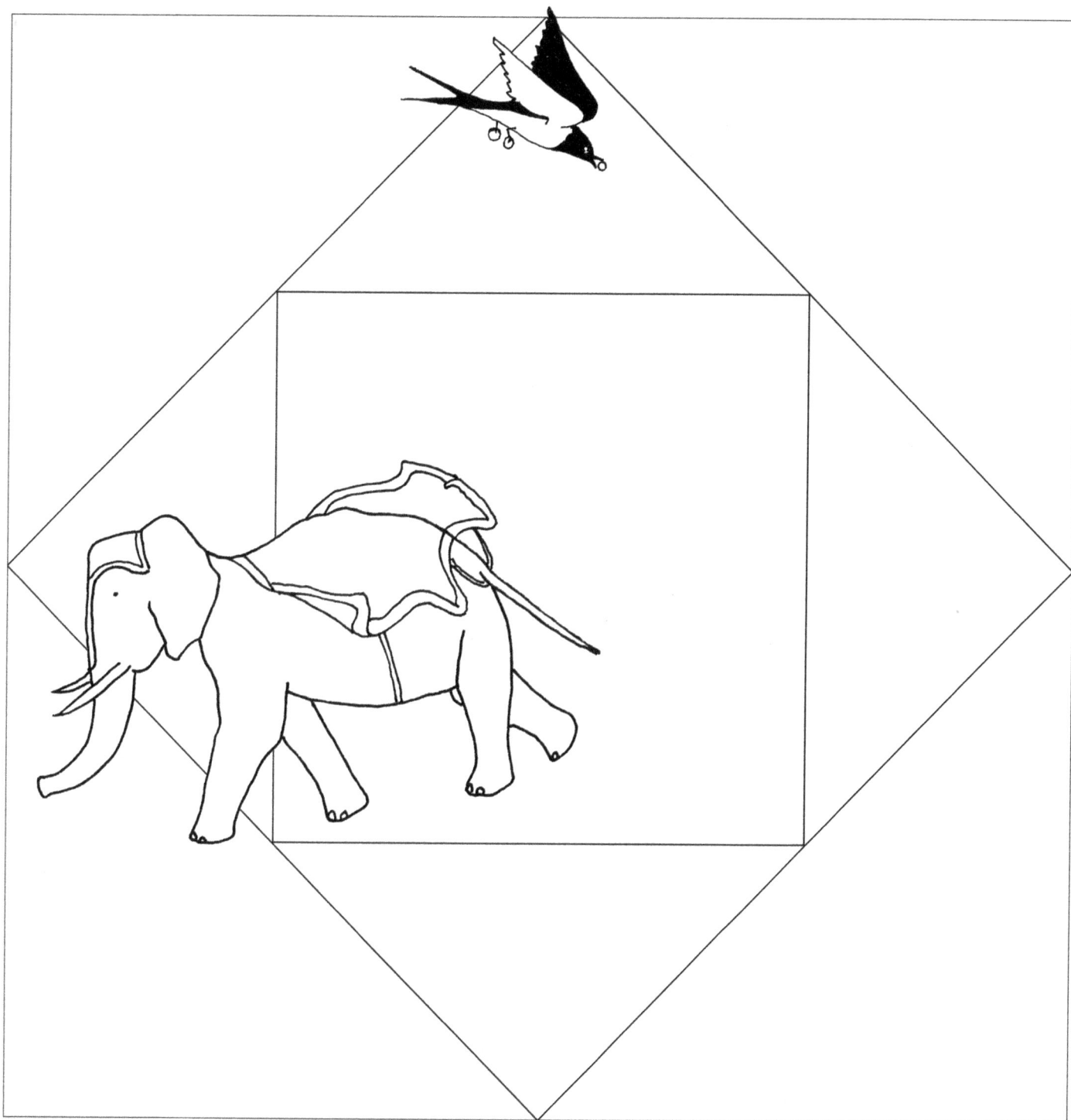

The Elephant of the Ka'ba

Could his small dark eyes see the heavenly light surrounding Mecca? Did his large sensitive ears hear a divine command to be still? Did a strong angelic hand keep his body stretched on the ground? Did his big believing heart simply refuse to do wrong?

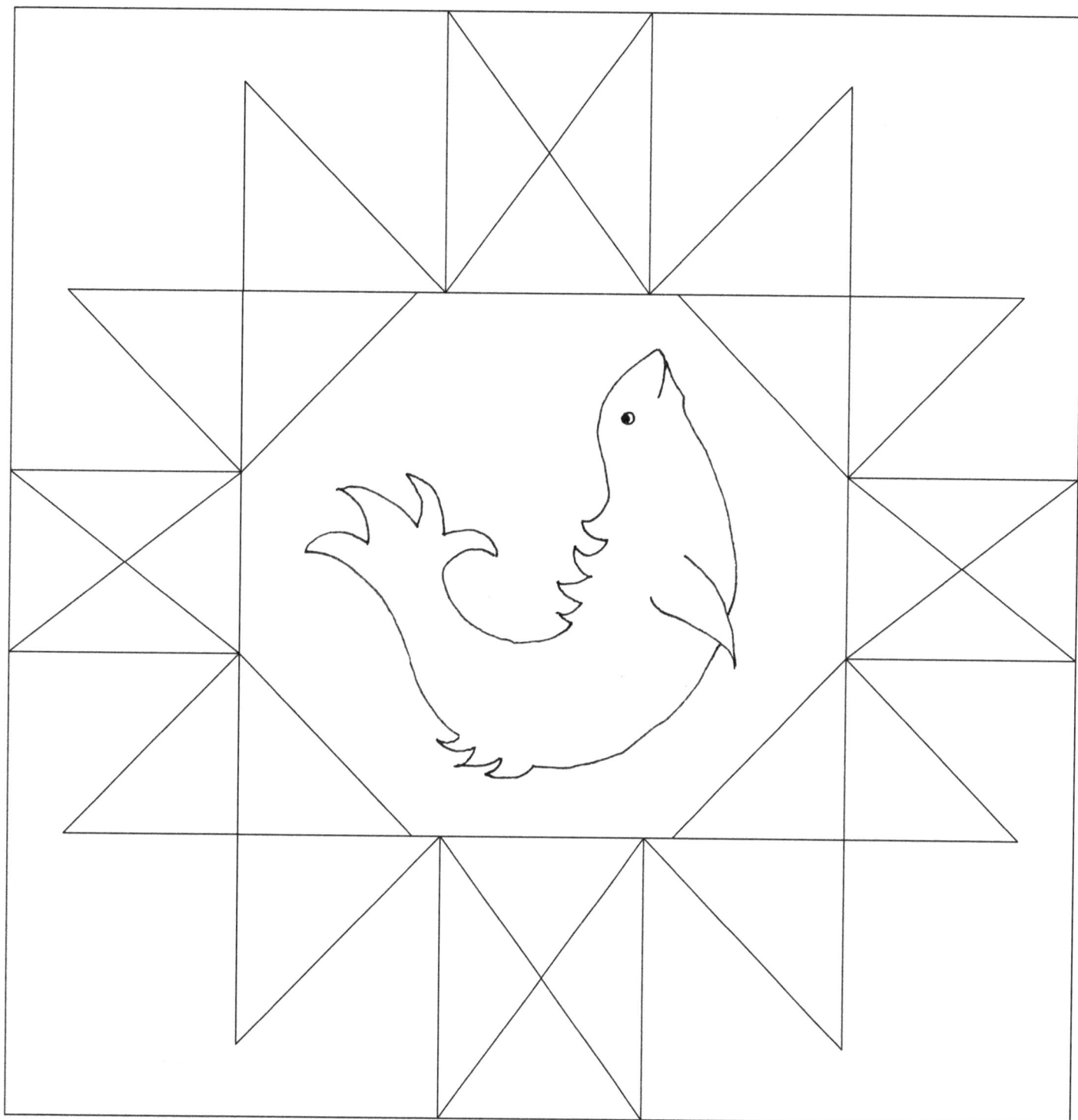

The Fish at the Birth of Prophet Muhammad (sas)

A huge fish, maybe the same one that had swallowed Prophet Yunus, jumped in and out of the sea making tremendous waves until the whole sea and all that lived within it knew that something very special was happening that day.

The Buraq

A buraq is a heavenly horse. His legs are of coral, his feet of gold. His chest is of ruby, his back of pearl. His wings are ruby red and his tail is like a peacock. He holds his head high because he carried on his back the light of the worlds.

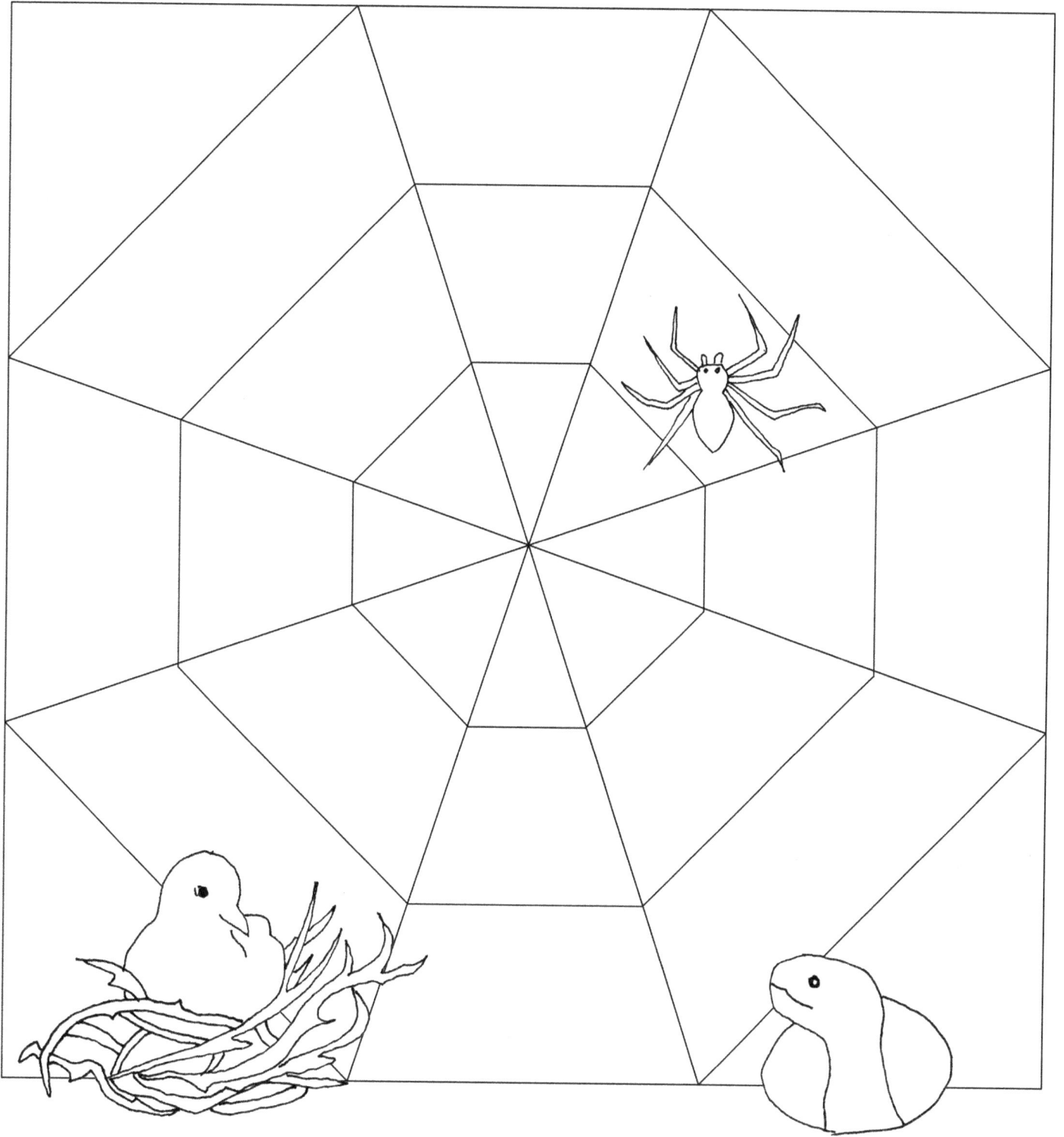

The Dove, the Spider, and the Snake of the Cave

With their love they kept the Prophet (sas) safe from his enemies.

The Riding Animals of the Prophet (sas)

They all served the Prophet Muhammad: Qaswa the rightly guided camel, Duldul the faithful mule, Ya'fur the intelligent donkey.

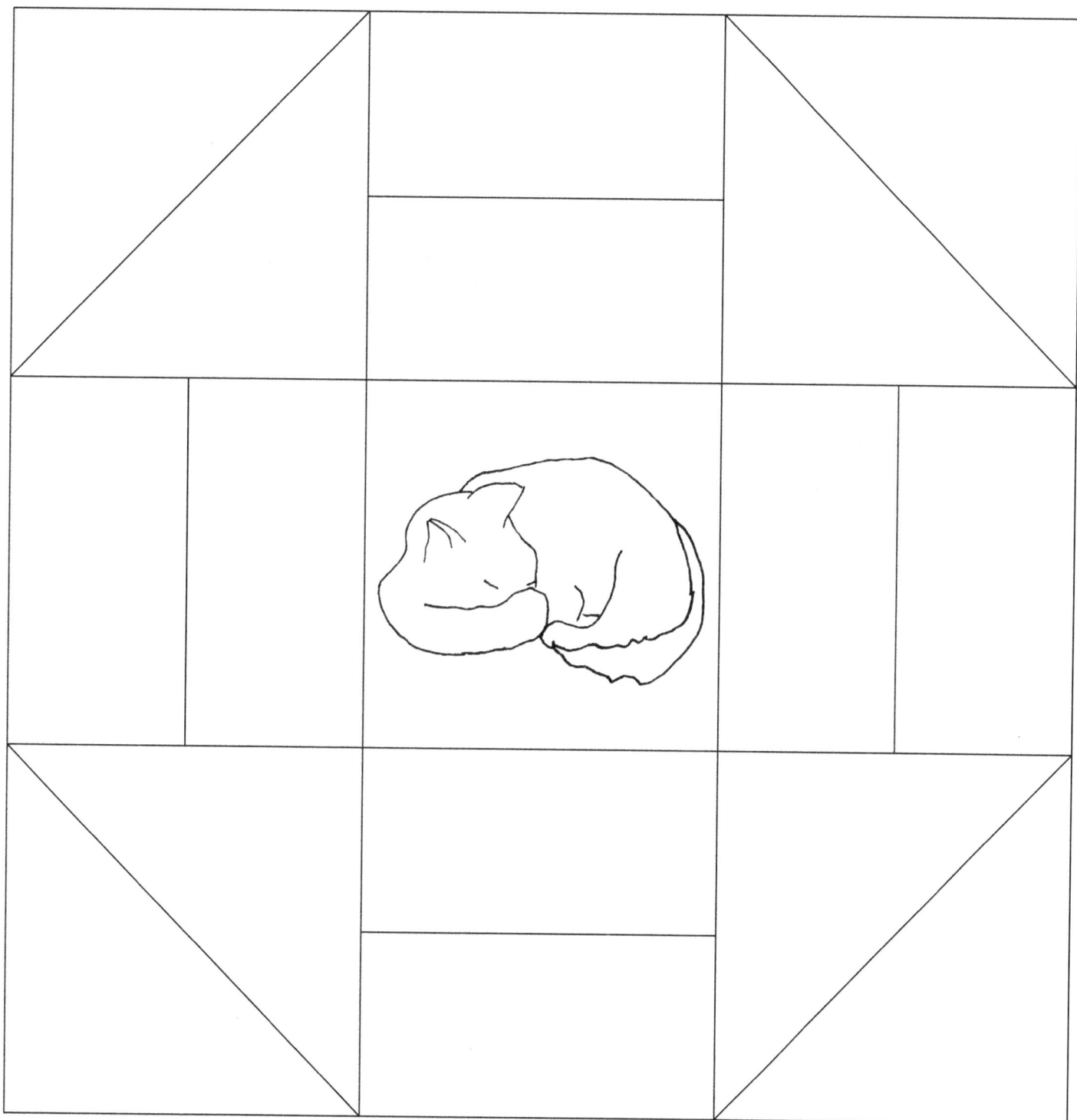

The Cat

The cat slept peacefully on the cloak of the Prophet (sas).

The Lizard

The lizard, while still hanging from the hunter's hands, said clearly in Arabic for all the people to hear, "La ilaha illa Allah, Muhammadun Rasulu Allah."

The Gazelle

She begged the merciful Prophet (sas) to let her go free for an hour so she could take her babies to a safer place.

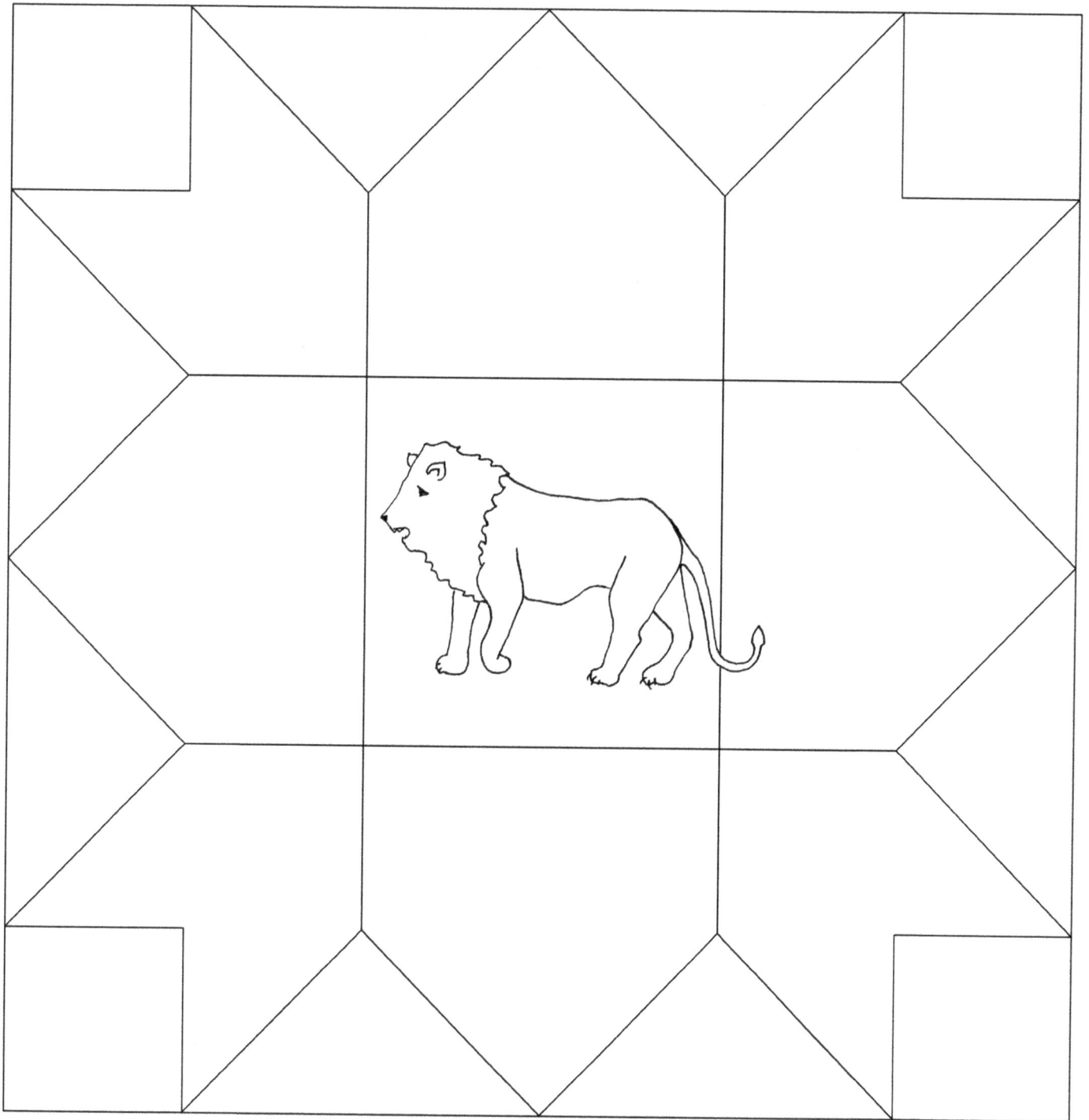

The Lion

The lion stood growling in his way and would not let him pass until he was pointed again in the right direction. All the way back to Medina, the lion kept the Prophet's companion company.

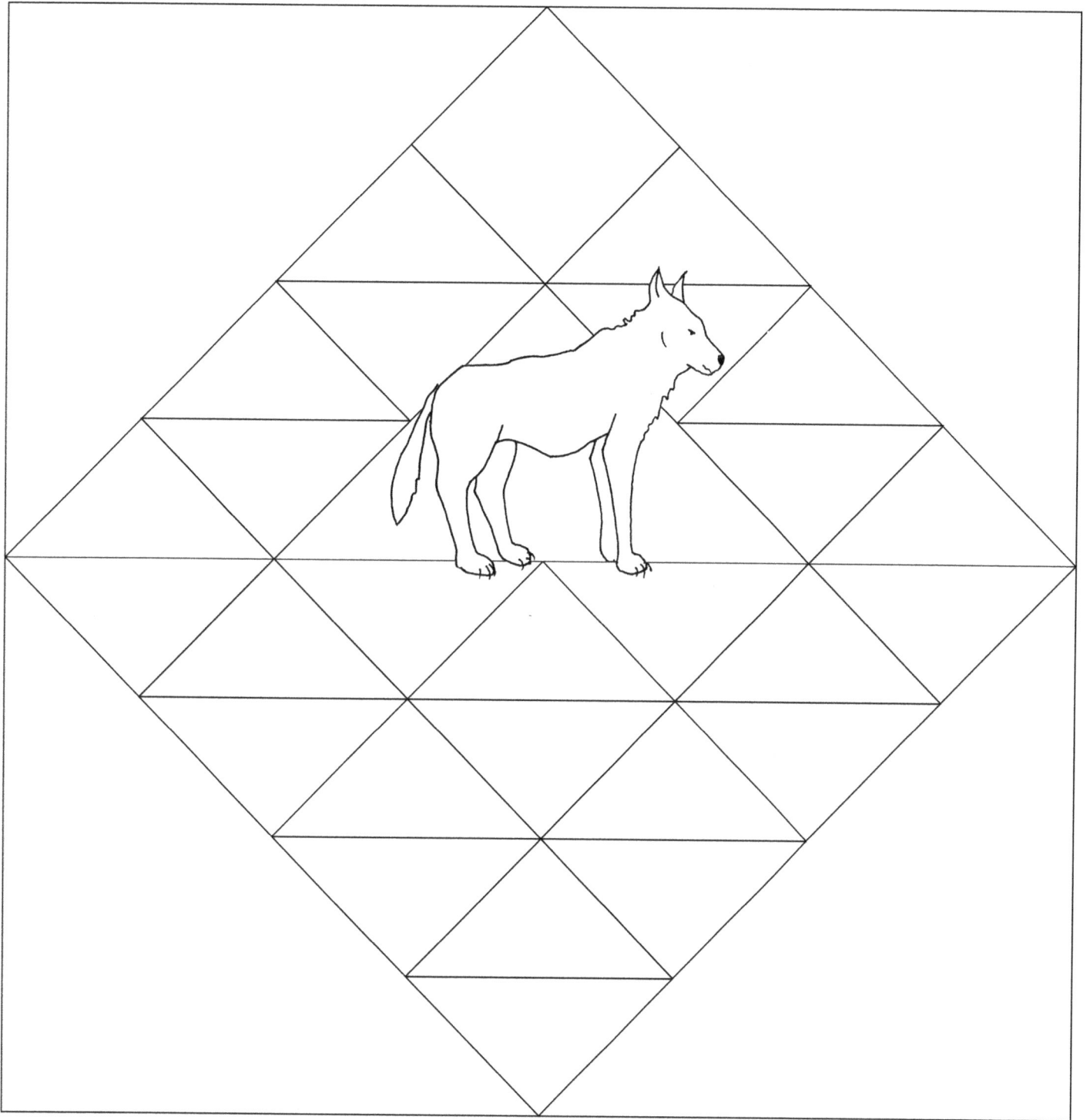

The Wolf

Putting his trust in the speaking wolf, Ahban (ra) went to visit the Prophet (sas). When he returned he found the wolf guarding his sheep safely where he had left them.

www.ingramcontent.com/pod-product-compliance
Lightning Source LLC
Chambersburg PA
CBHW080529030426
42337CB00023B/4679